FACT CAT

GHANA

Clare Hibbert

WAYLAND

FACT CAT

Get your paws on this fantastic new mega-series from Wayland!

Join our Fact Cat on a journey of fun learning about every subject under the sun!

First published in 2014 by Wayland
© Wayland 2014

Wayland
Hachette Children's Books
338 Euston Road
London NW1 3BH

Wayland Australia
Level 17/207 Kent Street
Sydney NSW 2000

Produced for Wayland by
White-Thomson Publishing Ltd
www.wtpub.co.uk
+44 (0) 843 208 7460

Editor: Clare Hibbert
Design: Rocket Design (East Anglia) Ltd
Fact Cat illustrations: Shutterstock/Julien Troneur
Other illustrations: Stefan Chabluk
Consultant: Kate Ruttle

A catalogue for this title is available from the British Library

ISBN: 978 0 7502 8215 4
ebook ISBN: 978 0 7502 8829 3

Dewey Number: 966.7–dc23

10 9 8 7 6 5 4 3 2 1

Wayland is a division of Hachette Children's Books,
an Hachette UK company.
www.hachette.co.uk

Printed and bound in China

Picture and illustration credits:
Chabluk, Stefan: 4; Corbis: Frans Lanting cover, Frans Lanting 8; Dreamstime: Aprescindere 1, Marcin Bartosz Czarnoleski 5, Marcin Bartosz Czarnoleski 9, Guppyimages 10, Marcin Bartosz Czarnoleski 13, Roejoe 20, Marcin Bartosz Czarnoleski 22; Getty: Tom Cockrem/Lonely Planet Images 6, Luca Sage/Photonica World 19, Jamie Squire/FIFA 21; Shutterstock: Pixel Europe cover map, Anton_Ivanov 7, Paul D Smith 15, Paul D Smith 16, Linda Hughes 17, fstockfoto 18; Thinkstock: Fuse 12; TopFoto: RIA Novosti 14; Wikimedia: benketaro 11.

Every effort has been made to clear copyright.
Should there be any inadvertent omission,
please apply to the publisher for rectification.

The author, Clare Hibbert, is a writer and editor specialising in children's information books.

The consultant, Kate Ruttle, is a literacy expert and SENCO, and teaches in Suffolk.

FACT CAT FACT

There is a question for you to answer on each spread in this book. You can check your answers on page 24.

CONTENTS

WELCOME TO GHANA

Ghana is a country in West Africa. It is close to the **equator**, so it is very hot all year round. It has a long **coastline**.

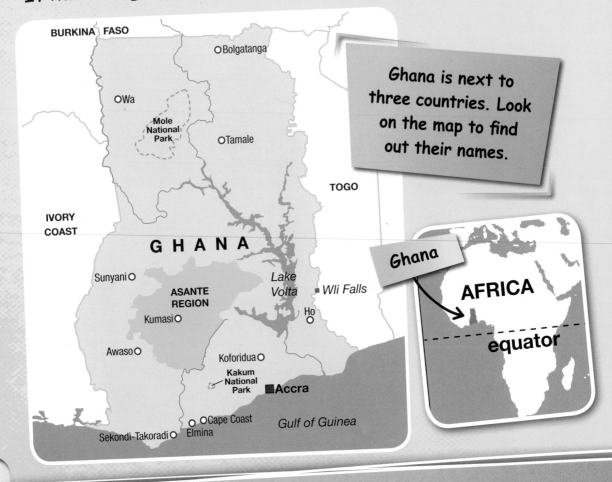

Ghana is next to three countries. Look on the map to find out their names.

BURKINA FASO

○ Bolgatanga

○ Wa

Mole National Park

○ Tamale

TOGO

IVORY COAST

G H A N A

Sunyani ○

ASANTE REGION

Kumasi ○

Awaso ○

Lake Volta

■ Wli Falls

Ho ○

Koforidua ○

Kakum National Park

■ Accra

○ Cape Coast

Sekondi-Takoradi ○ Elmina

Gulf of Guinea

Ghana

AFRICA

equator

Ghana has more than 100 different **tribes**. A tribe is a group of people who have their own language and beliefs. One tribe, the **Ashanti**, grew rich selling gold to people from other countries.

These market boats are in busy Elmina. The town has been a **trading post** for hundreds of years.

NYAME BEK

FACT CAT FACT

Ghana used to be called the Gold Coast because of the trade in gold. It was named 'Ghana' about 65 years ago.

CITIES AND VILLAGES

Ghana's capital city is Accra. More than two million people live in and around the city. There are lots of street markets.

Accra is large and bustling, but a city in the Asante region is even bigger. Find out what its name is.

About half of all **Ghanaians** live in towns or cities. The other half live in villages in the countryside and work on farms. Most Ghanaian farmers only grow enough food to feed themselves and their families.

Villagers live in mud houses with thatched grass roofs.

FACT CAT FACT

Ghana has some large farms that grow **crops** for sale. Cocoa beans are the biggest crop. They are used to make chocolate.

THE LAND

Part of Ghana is covered by **rainforest**. It is hot and steamy and rain falls every day. Some forest has been chopped down to make way for farms or **mines**.

This is Kakum **National Park**, where the rainforest cannot be cut down. Find out how many national parks Ghana has.

FACT CAT FACT

Ghana's tallest waterfall is in the rainforest. The Wli Waterfall is 143 metres high.

Ghana has the world's largest **reservoir**. Lake Volta covers more than 8,500 sq km. The lake provides water for farmers' fields. It is full of fish that people can catch and sell.

These villagers worked together to net fish. They are sharing them out.

FOOD

Fufu is a favourite dish in Ghana. It looks like a white sticky ball. You pinch off a bit in your fingers and dip it into some spicy soup.

Fufu is made by pounding boiled **yam** or **cassava** with **plantain**. Find out why it is called 'fufu'.

Ghanaians enjoy fried fish and chicken, along with stews or rice and beans. 'Red red' is a special dish of bean stew and fried plantain.

Red red gets its name from the orangey-red colours of the stew and the fried plantain.

FACT CAT FACT

Ghanaians like spicy food. *Shito* is a popular sauce made from chilli peppers, ginger and dried shrimps.

WILDLIFE

Ghana is home to many amazing wild animals. There are lions and leopards, elephants and hippos. There are also monkeys, baboons and bushbabies.

The leopard lives in forests and grasslands. It is a fierce hunter. Can you find out what its spots are called?

Wild pigs called warthogs live on the grasslands. During the wet season, they feed on grass. In the dry season, they dig up bulbs and roots.

A warthog has two pairs of tusks for digging and fighting. The bottom ones are short but very sharp.

FACT CAT FACT

Warthogs are named for the warty bumps on their heads.

CELEBRATIONS

Family is important in Ghana. When someone dies, the whole family comes together to say goodbye. People are buried in colourful coffins.

This carpenter is painting a coffin which is shaped like a fish!

FACT CAT FACT

People's coffins say something about their life. Someone who worked as a fisherman might be buried in a fish-shaped coffin.

Adae Kese is a big Ashanti festival. People remember the dead and spring-clean their houses. They parade a golden throne through the streets. There is drumming and dancing.

The Ashanti king wears all his gold at Adae Kesi. Find out the Ashanti word for 'king'.

CRAFT

The Ashanti people are famous for their bright *kente* cloth. They make it by weaving together strips of silk and cotton. Each pattern has a different meaning.

Today, anyone can buy *kente* cloth. Long ago, only certain people could wear it. Find out who.

Ghanaian people make masks from leather, metal or wood. Masks such as these have been used for thousands of years.

People believed that wearing a mask helped them talk to **spirits**.

Ghanaians sometimes carve animals on their masks. The animals all mean something. Birds mean hope.

SPORT

Football is the best-loved sport in Ghana. The biggest local teams are Asante Kotoko SC and Accra Hearts of Oak SC.

Fans cheer as Ghana scores in a World Cup match. The national team is called the Black Stars. Find out why.

Boxing is another popular sport. Bukom, a part of Accra, is famous for its boxers. It has around 20 **boxing gyms**.

Two boys box on a street in Bukom. Perhaps they dream of being the next world champion!

FACT CAT FACT

The boxer Azumah Nelson is a national hero in Ghana. He was world champion three times!

FAMOUS PEOPLE

Kofi Annan is the most famous Ghanaian in the world. He was the leader of the **United Nations** from 1997 to 2006.

Kofi Annan worked hard to stop wars and bring peace. Find out which year he won the **Nobel Peace Prize**.

FACT CAT FACT

The United Nations was set up in 1945 after the end of the Second World War.

Derek Boateng is a world-class football player from Accra. He plays as **midfielder** for Ghana's national team. He is also midfielder for Fulham in England's **Premier League**.

Derek Boateng played for his country in the 2010 World Cup. Ghana reached the quarter-finals.

QUIZ

Try to answer the questions below. Look back through the book to help you. Check your answers on page 24.

1 Which of these big cats does not live in Ghana?

a) leopard

b) lion

c) jaguar

2 What is Ghana's biggest crop?

a) cocoa beans

b) coconuts

c) pineapples

3 'Blue blue' is a popular Ghanaian stew. True or not true?

a) true

b) not true

4 What is the name of Ghana's huge artificial lake?

a) Lake Volta

b) Lake Malta

c) Lake Walter

5 Elmina is the capital of Ghana. True or not true?

a) true

b) not true

GLOSSARY

Ashanti a people who live in Ghana and Ivory Coast. They share a language, called Akan, and many customs and traditions. Their king is called the Asantehene.

boxing gym a club where boxers go to train

capital the city where the government (the group of people who lead a country) meets

carpenter someone who makes things out of wood for a living

cassava a starchy root vegetable that is eaten in the tropics

coastline a stretch of land next to the sea

crop a plant that farmers grow, usually for food

equator an imaginary line around the middle of the Earth at the same distance from the North and South Poles

Ghanaian someone from Ghana

midfielder a footballer who plays in the middle of the pitch, between the attackers and the defenders

mine a place where people dig useful substances out of the ground, such as coal, copper or gold

national park an area where the landscape is protected by law so it stays wild

Nobel Peace Prize a yearly award, given to a person or organisation that has worked hard for peace in the world

plantain a fruit related to bananas that has to be cooked before eating

Premier League a group of English football clubs that compete against each other during the football season from August to May

rainforest a thick, tropical forest where there are heavy rains almost every day

reservoir a lake that has been made by people

spirit an invisible being, often thought to have magical powers

trading post a place where people go to buy and sell goods

tribe a group of families that live together and share the same language and customs

United Nations an organisation of countries that work together to stop wars

yam a starchy root vegetable that is an important food. Almost all the world's yams are grown in West Africa.

INDEX

ANSWERS

Pages 4–20

page 4: The countries are Ivory Coast, Burkina Faso and Togo.

page 6: Kumasi, the capital of the Asante region.

page 8: Ghana has seven national parks.

page 10: The word 'fufu' is meant to sound like the pounding sound when the ingredients are mashed up.

page 12: The spots are called rosettes.

page 15: The king is known as the 'Asantehene'. The one in the picture is Osei Tutu II, who became king in 1999.

page 16: Only members of the royal family could wear *kente* cloth.

page 18: The players' kit features the same black star that appears on Ghana's national flag.

page 20: Kofi Annan won the Nobel Peace Prize in 2001. He shared it with the United Nations.

Quiz answers

1   c)

2   a)

3   b)

4   a)

5   b)

OTHER TITLES IN THE FACT CAT SERIES...

SPACE

978 0 7502 8221 5

978 0 7502 8223 9

978 0 7502 8222 2

978 0 7502 8220 8

UNITED KINGDOM

978 0 7502 8433 2

978 0 7502 8439 4

978 0 7502 8440 0

978 0 7502 8438 7

HISTORY

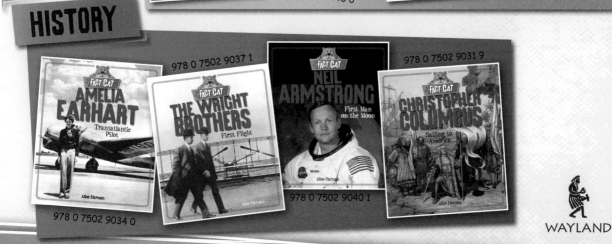

978 0 7502 9037 1

978 0 7502 9031 9

978 0 7502 9040 1

978 0 7502 9034 0

WAYLAND